IMAGES
of America

FORBES FIELD

ON THE COVER: An aerial view of Forbes Field shows a packed crowd to see the Pirates play on a splendid summer afternoon. Throughout the stadium's remarkable 61-year run, millions of Western Pennsylvania natives flocked to this legendary facility to not only see the best baseball had to offer, but football and boxing too. Its run came to an end on June 28, 1970, when the Pirates closed its doors with a 4-1 victory over the Cubs. (Courtesy of the Pittsburgh Pirates.)

IMAGES
of America

FORBES FIELD

David Finoli and Thomas Aikens

ARCADIA
PUBLISHING

Published by Arcadia Publishing
Charleston, South Carolina

Printed in the United States of America

Library of Congress Control Number: 2012947319

For all general information, please contact Arcadia Publishing:
Telephone 843-853-2070
Fax 843-853-0044
E-mail sales@arcadiapublishing.com
For customer service and orders:
Toll-Free 1-888-313-2665

Visit us on the Internet at www.arcadiapublishing.com

To Mary Salsie, who had a joy in life and the desire to help those who needed it. She helped shape the lives we lead today.

CONTENTS

ACKNOWLEDGMENTS

To complete any project requires the help and support of many people; this one was no different.

To begin, the authors would like to thank their families. Dave's wife, Vivian, whom he has been happily married to for 27 years, and his three children—Cara, Matthew, and Tony—have provided him with the great life he lives today right outside of Pittsburgh in Monroeville, Pennsylvania. Also, Dave would like to thank his mother, Eleanor, sister Mary, brother Jamie, nieces Brianna and Marissa, as well as his father, Domenic, who enjoyed many memorable moments inside Forbes Field; and, while he once confided to us that it smelled like urine and stale beer, at 97 years old, he still misses it to this day.

Tom would like to thank his children—Elizabeth, Ben, and Catherine—whom he enjoys his life with in the wonderful city of Greensburg, Pennsylvania. He would also like to thank his sisters Amanda and Claudia as well as his mother, Evelyn, in loving memory, and father, Tom, who helped shape his life.

The authors would also like to acknowledge those for whom this project would not have been a reality, including the following people who generously contributed the photographs. Jim Trdinich of the Pittsburgh Pirates has helped the authors on this as well as many other projects they have undertaken. EJ Borghetti, senior associate athletic director/media relations for the University of Pittsburgh, has always given his time without question, whether it is for photographs or research. Thanks go to Dave Saba, the associate athletic director/media relations for Dave's alma mater, Duquesne University. Thanks go to Scott McGuinness, the fine sports information director at Washington and Jefferson College. And thanks are extended to Tim Conn, the son of the legendary light-heavyweight champion of the world Bill Conn, who donated photographs of his father.

Finally, the authors would like to acknowledge and thank Abby Henry and the wonderful people at Arcadia Publishing who make this, as well as every project the authors have done with them, a pure joy.

Those photographs without courtesy lines are courtesy of the Pittsburgh Pirates.

INTRODUCTION

As the first decade of the 20th century was coming to a close, the Pittsburgh Pirates became arguably the most successful franchise in the National League. They also played in one of the worst facilities in the circuit, Exposition Park.

Their home since 1891, Exposition Park had seen three National League championships (1901–1903) and had also seen more than its share of flooding. The outfield, located right off of Pittsburgh's three rivers, would often be flooded, sometimes necessitating special ground rules.

Pirate president Barney Dreyfuss, sick of the constant water issues, decided to move inland, to the Oakland section of the city to build the National League's first stadium of steel and concrete. While historians would concur that the flooding was the major reason Dreyfuss wanted to build his new facility, others felt it was because Oakland, which is the section of the city where the University of Pittsburgh was built, was a more affluent area as opposed to the "North Side"; the location of Exposition Park was a much rowdier part of town.

Regardless of the reason, construction began on March 1, 1909, to be completed by midseason. Many mocked Dreyfuss when he announced his magnificent new stadium would seat 25,000 patrons. They called the planned ballpark "Dreyfuss's Folly." One opposing team owner bet him he would never fill the park. Dreyfuss won the bet the first time a game was played there. Amid much fanfare, including a parade featuring past ballplayers who lived locally, the Pirates played and lost their first game at Forbes Field, 3-2, before 30,338 people on June 30, 1909. Dreyfuss chose the name Forbes Field to honor British general John Forbes, who had fought a battle with the French for Fort Duquesne during the French and Indian War in 1758. Although the French burned the fort, the British erected Fort Pitt nearby, which became the cornerstone of a new city—Pittsburgh.

Forbes Field became the sports cornerstone of the city; it was truly a sight to behold. The dimensions of the ballpark were huge, with its deepest point in left center field originally a distance of 462 feet from home plate. The left field line was 360 feet away, and right field was 400 feet away. A drive to dead center would have to travel 447 feet to reach the wall. A big ballpark for the players, Forbes was also a grand ballpark for its spectators. It was one of the first ballparks to include inclined ramps instead of stairs to the upper deck, private luxury boxes, and an area for the press on the third level.

Those who entered the facility over the next 61 years would be privy to some of the city's most magical moments. The greats of the Negro League played on its rocky infield as the Homestead Grays called it home until they moved to Washington, DC, later in the team's existence. During its early days, Forbes Field was the epicenter of college football as three of the cities universities played there while enjoying success on the national level. Before moving to Pitt Stadium, the University of Pittsburgh football program won three national championships in 1915, 1916, and 1919. Duquesne University had one of the country's premier programs between 1934 and 1941, while Carnegie Tech (now Carnegie Mellon University) defeated Knute Rockne's powerhouse

Notre Dame squad in 1926 at Forbes Field and had a surprising 1938 campaign where the team finished sixth in the nation and went to the Sugar Bowl.

In the days before becoming the preeminent team in the National Football League, winning six-Super Bowl championships, the Pittsburgh Steelers began their tenure as the Pittsburgh Pirates in 1933 and played in Forbes. While there was some success, including their first postseason experience in 1947 where they lost the Eastern Division title to the Philadelphia Eagles 21-0, most of their time in Forbes was spent at the bottom of the standings. They toiled in Forbes Field until they moved to Pitt Stadium in 1963.

Forbes Field also played host to many of boxing's greats, including Harry Greb, Billy Conn, Fritzie Zivic, and the memorable Ezzard Charles-Jersey Joe Walcott heavyweight championship bout in 1951. One of the most unique stories at the facility came during the famous 1941 Joe Louis–Billy Conn heavyweight championship fight that took place in 1941 at the Polo Grounds in New York. The Pirates were playing the Giants that night at Forbes Field, and when the fight began, they stopped the baseball game so the throng at Forbes could listen to their hometown hero almost pull one of the greatest upsets in the history of the sport. Besides boxing and football, there were nonathletic events, such as several religious and political gatherings, including a visit by William Howard Taft.

While there were many things that happened there, the main purpose was to house the city's professional baseball team, the Pirates, and in that respect, Forbes Field did its job very well. It saw Ralph Kiner become one of the most prestigious power hitters the game has ever seen. Large throngs would enter its gates despite the fact the Bucs were one of the worst teams in the league. Once Kiner had his last at bat, the crowd filtered onto the streets before the game was over.

From a World Series victory in its first season in 1909 to the great comeback in 1925 when Kiki Cuyler hit a double to beat the Senators 9-7 in game seven—and of course Bill Mazeroski's dramatic home run over the left field wall to beat the Yankees 10-9 in the 1960 World Series finale—Forbes Field has seen it all. It touched the hearts of all who passed through its gates, many of whom still revel in the memories as they celebrate the greatest moment ever seen within its walls—the 1960 World Series game seven victory against the Yankees, remembered annually with a rebroadcast of the classic contest on October 13 at the left center field wall that still remains as is today, a symbol of some of the greatest sports moments this town has ever seen.

One

1909

FROM FLOODS TO OAKLAND

1909 was a banner year for the Pittsburgh Pirates. In fact, it was the year they not only brought themselves into the modern era of baseball but also finally found a way to erase the stink of their upset loss in the 1903 World Series. The thing that made it even more exciting was that they were able to do this in a brand-new, state-of-the-art facility.

In the early part of the century's first decade, the Pirates were winning many National League pennants, but they were doing so in a park that flooded often, requiring many unique ground rules to make up for the sometimes watery outfield. Sick of the flooding as well as just wanting a park that could seat more patrons than Exposition Park could handle, Pirate president Barney Dreyfuss began to buy land in the more affluent Oakland section of the city, near Schenley Park.

In 1909, Dreyfuss started construction of what would be one of the most superb buildings the National League had ever seen. The first stadium in the Senior Circuit, built of steel and concrete and named after French and Indian War hero John Forbes, Forbes Field was opened on June 30, only 122 days after ground was broken.

While a sellout throng of 30,338 watched the Bucs lose to the Chicago Cubs 3-2 that day, it was not exactly a foreshadowing of things to come. It had been six years since the Bucs last made an appearance in the World Series, but Forbes Field would prove to be a good luck charm in its first year of existence as it was the backdrop to a magical season. Pittsburgh would host the Detroit Tigers in the 1909 Fall Classic, a memorable series where two of the greatest players ever to take the diamond, the Pirates' Honus Wagner and the Tigers' Ty Cobb, faced each other in the first World Series to go to a deciding game, with the Pirates winning the initial World Series title in the history of the franchise. It was a perfect way to open the 61-year tenure of this magnificent stadium.

Pictured is the home of the Pittsburgh Pirates from 1891–1909, Exposition Park, which was located on the North Side of Pittsburgh right between where PNC Park and Heinz Field stand today. It hosted three championship squads in its short tenure, but unfortunately, it often flooded. This was perhaps the major reason Pirate president Barney Dreyfuss took his club to the Oakland section of Pittsburgh, where, in 1909, he opened the first ballpark in the National League that was built primarily of steel and concrete. He would call his new stadium Forbes Field, after French and Indian War hero Gen. John Forbes. The stadium was located nowhere near water, solving the problem of flooding.

This view from Schenley Park shows Forbes Field in its infancy. It is apparent in the photograph that the Pirates had yet to build their signature right field stands as well as the brick, ivy-covered wall. Helped by the renowned philanthropist and industrialist Andrew Carnegie, Pirates president Barney Dreyfuss purchased seven acres of land right next to the famed Pittsburgh Park in order to build his new stadium. Dreyfuss said that he was committed to "make the ballpark . . . of a design that would harmonize with the other structures in the Schenley Park district." (Courtesy of Library of Congress, Prints and Photographs Division, 4a19419r.)

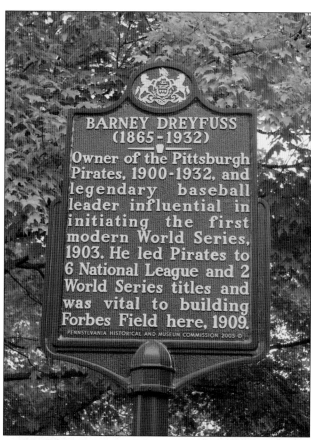

Pictured here is the Pennsylvania State Historical Marker that honors Barney Dreyfuss, who presided over the franchise during its most successful decade between 1900 and 1909, when it won four National League crowns and a World Series championship. The marker is located in the Oakland section of the city, where he gave Pittsburgh his greatest present, Forbes Field. (Courtesy of David Finoli.)

Pictured with his fellow National League owners and officers, Barney Dreyfuss (fourth from the left in the top row) was considered not only an innovative owner, but also one of the best scouts, "discovering more great players than any man in the game," according to NL president John Heydler (to the right of Dreyfuss). (Courtesy of Library of Congress, Prints and Photographs Division, LC-B2- 2701-16.)

Elected to the Hall of Fame in 1945, Fred Clarke is one of the few major leaguers with credentials to enter the halls of Cooperstown as both a player and manager. He hit .312 with 2,678 hits, while guiding the Bucs to a 1,422-969 record, four National League titles, and a world championship in the 1909 Fall Classic as a manager.

Generally considered the greatest player ever to don a Pittsburgh Pirate uniform, shortstop Honus Wagner hit .328 with 3,420 hits. A hometown boy from nearby Carnegie, Pennsylvania, Wagner came to the Pirates in 1900 from the Louisville Colonels when the Colonels were contracted from the league in 1899. Wagner came over with Fred Clarke and several other players that made the Pirates baseball's first great dynasty of the 1900s.

Deacon Phillippe was another important player who came to the Bucs from the Louisville Colonels in 1900. A control pitcher who walked only 1.25 batters per nine innings, Phillippe won 20 games in each of his first four seasons with the club. His most memorable victory of note was as the first pitcher ever to win a World Series game, in 1903.

Nick Maddox is known in Pirate lore as the first player ever to pitch a no-hitter for the franchise. He tossed his gem after being a late-season call-up by Pittsburgh, beating Brooklyn 2-1 in 1907. Maddox was 13-8 in 1909 and was the winning pitcher against Detroit in game three of the 1909 World Series. His star was fleeting, as he was out of the majors by 1911.

Pictured here is the fountain, now located in Schenley Park, that used to overlook Forbes Field. Schenley Park was built in 1889 after 300 acres were donated to the city by Mary Croghan Schenley. It has been developed extensively over the years and in 2011 was named one of "America's Coolest Parks" by *Travel + Leisure* magazine. (Courtesy of David Finoli.)

Pirates president Barney Dreyfuss contracted famed architect and engineer Charles Wellford Leavitt Jr. to create his new facility, Forbes Field. Leavitt had designed such famous racetracks as Belmont Park and Saratoga Raceway, had been invited to submit a plan by Dreyfuss (who loved to gamble on the horses), and had been to Belmont Park in the past.

Pictured is the crowd coming from Schenley Park into Forbes Field on horse-drawn carriages for the facility's opening day on June 30, 1909, a game against the defending world champion Chicago Cubs. Some 30,338 stuffed themselves into the 25,000-seat stadium to see the Cubs win 3-2. It would be one of the few down moments at Forbes Field in 1909 for the Pirates.

This is the view of Forbes Field down the left field line when it first opened in 1909. The *1910 Reach Baseball Guide* says, "For architectural beauty, imposing size, solid construction and public comfort and convenience, it has not its superior in the world." (Courtesy of Library of Congress, Prints and Photographs Division, LC-D4-15637 L.)

Nicknamed "Wee" because of his diminutive five-foot-six-inch, 135-pound frame, Tommy Leach nonetheless was an important part of the Pirates championship run in the first decade of the 20th century. The .269 lifetime hitter is known in baseball history by getting the first hit in the World Series, a triple, and scoring the Fall Classic's first run, both in 1903. (Courtesy of Library of Congress, Prints and Photographs Division, LC-B2- 2210-5.)

Moving to a more spacious Forbes Field from Exposition Park (pictured), Barney Dreyfuss had 8,000 additional temporary bleachers installed for the 1909 World Series at the new home. The demand for tickets was larger than the supply, as he had to return over $100,000 of ticket requests that he could not fill. (Courtesy of Library of Congress, Prints and Photographs Division, 6a29695.)

Pictured are the 1909 National League Champion Pittsburgh Pirates. Winners of what still remains a club record 110 games, Pittsburgh won the pennant over the defending world champion Chicago Cubs by 6.5 games. Led by Hall of Famer Honus Wagner (pictured in the bottom row to the left of the bat), who hit .339 to capture his seventh National League batting crown, the Bucs led the

league with a .260 average, scoring 701 runs, a full 69 runs more than the second-best team. It was a great season for their first in Forbes Field, which proved to be very fortuitous for the Bucs. After losing three of the first four in their new facility, they finished the year 37-16 at Forbes.

By 1909, Hall of Famer Fred Clarke's career was coming to an end. The 36-year-old left fielder still had a fine season, hitting .287, but had a less than stellar series with a .211 average. While he was not at his best, Clarke nonetheless led the Fall Classic with two home runs, one in game one and the second in the fifth contest—both Pirate victories.

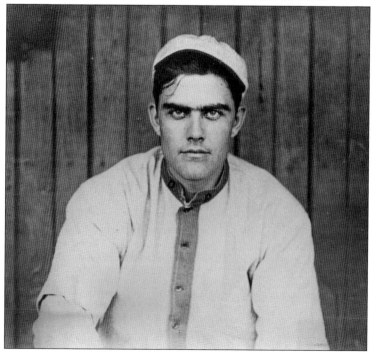

Despite the fact he was 12-3 with a miniscule 1.11 ERA, Babe Adams was the surprise starter for the Pirates in game one of the 1909 World Series at Forbes Field. The move by manager Fred Clarke proved to be genius, as he went on not only to win that contest 4-1 but also two other games, including an 8-0 shutout in game seven to give the Pirates the title.

The demand for tickets to the 1909 World Series in Pittsburgh was so thorough that people would do anything to catch a glimpse of the action. In this photograph, fans climb a pole to see the Pirates at Forbes Field. Over 81,000 fans attended the three games in Pittsburgh for the series, a record at the time. (Courtesy of Library of Congress, Prints and Photographs Division, LC-USZ62-103768.)

The most interesting story of the 1909 World Series was the matchup between two of the greatest players in the history of the game, Pittsburgh's Honus Wagner (center) and Detroit's Ty Cobb (far right), comparing bats at Forbes Field before the first game. It was a classic matchup of good (Wagner) versus evil (Cobb) that made the encounter so intriguing. (Courtesy of Library of Congress, Prints and Photographs Division, LC-USZ62-103768.)

Considered the consummate sportsman, Honus Wagner had the worst moment in his Hall of Fame career six years earlier, hitting only .222 in the Bucs loss in the 1903 World Series. In this Fall Classic, he more than made up for it with a .333 average and six RBIs, leading Pittsburgh to its first world championship.

The bad boy in this matchup, Detroit's Ty Cobb had to take a roundabout way, traveling through Canada and then down to Pittsburgh to avoid Ohio policemen who were looking to arrest him for an incident in Cleveland earlier in the season. The extensive travel took its toll on Cobb, as he hit only .231 in the Detroit loss. (Courtesy of Library of Congress, Prints and Photographs Division, LC-DIG-ggbain-08006.)

Two

1910–1930
National Championships and World Series

As the Pirates entered their first full decade in Forbes Field, a funny thing happened: they no longer were the most successful tenants in the building.

After capturing their first World Series championship in the inaugural season of Forbes Field, the Bucs quickly aged as players like Honus Wagner, Fred Clarke, and Deacon Phillippe were replaced by much less prominent ones, such as Joe Kelly, Chuck Ward, and Marty O'Toole. The result was a sequence of seasons that saw the club finish in the bottom half of the league between 1914 and 1918. Thankfully for the Forbes Field patrons, there was the football team that represented the University of Pittsburgh to stoke their championship hopes.

In 1915, one of the greatest coaches to ever grace the sidelines on a college football gridiron, Glenn "Pop" Warner, took over the controls of the Pitt Panther football program. The results were immediately staggering. Warner went 8-0 his first season and won his first 30 games as the Panther coach, capturing three national championships in 1915, 1916, and 1918.

Warner's teams continued to dazzle opponents at Forbes until 1923, when he turned the program over to his protégé, Jock Sutherland. Sutherland continued the success, but he did so at Pitt Stadium, as the school opened up its own football-only facility in 1925.

Again, Forbes Field fans were lucky as by 1925, Pittsburgh was again on top of the baseball world, bringing the second Fall Classic to the legendary stadium that same season. It was an exciting series that saw Pittsburgh become the first team ever to recover from a three-games-to one deficit to win the championship, with an exciting contest in game seven as Kiki Cuyler hit an eighth-inning double to give Pittsburgh a 9-7 win at a rain-soaked Forbes Field.

Two years later, they captured their sixth National League crown, bringing the series again to Pittsburgh. This time, unfortunately, they were swept by the Yankees.

Despite the loss, the first 31 seasons at Forbes Field were truly special, and the titles won within its walls made it the house of champions.

This aerial view shows Forbes Field and Schenley Park soon after it was built. The park was donated to the city by Mary Schenley and today covers over 456 acres. Presently, some of the things that are found within its borders include the Phipps Conservatory, a swimming pool, an ice rink, an all-weather track, soccer fields, and an 18-hole disc golf course.

For the opening of the 1925 season, Forbes Field had its first significant change when Barney Dreyfuss had a grandstand built that extended down the remainder of the first base line around to right field; the new grandstand reduced the dimensions of the park in right field from 376 feet to a more manageable 300. (Courtesy of Library of Congress, Prints and Photographs Division, LC-D4-15634 L.)

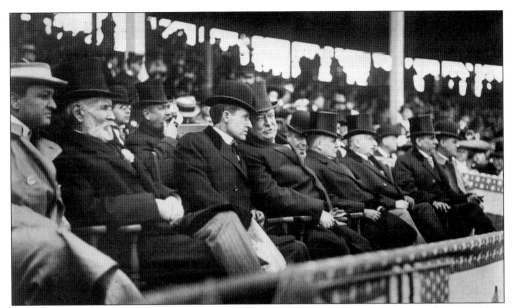

In 1909, on one of his many trips to Pittsburgh, Pres. William Howard Taft attended one of the final games at Exposition Park before it gave way to Forbes Field, when the Bucs lost to the Cubs 8-3, their only loss in 19 games. Another was in Forbes Field as Taft was a guest at the first Mine Safety Demonstration and International Safety Conference, which was held at the stadium in 1911. There were many other state and federal officials on hand, along with over 15,000 spectators, as the miners from every coal-mining state, trained in first aid and rescue work, took part in the demonstration. (Courtesy of Library of Congress, Prints and Photographs Division, LC-USZ62-122411&LC-DIG-ggbain-08019.)

One of the early configurations of Forbes Field included these temporary stands, built in left field to allow more patrons to view such memorable events as the opening of the park on June 30, 1909, and the 1909 World Series, when the Pirates won their first world championship. (Courtesy of Library of Congress, Prints and Photographs Division, LC-D4-15634.)

As the Pirates starting falling in the standings in the mid-1910s, Pittsburgh sports fans had another team to pin their championship hopes on, the University of Pittsburgh football team. Pictured is head coach Glenn "Pop" Warner. One of the greatest coaches in the history of the game, Warner brought three national championships to Forbes Field. (Courtesy of the University of Pittsburgh.)

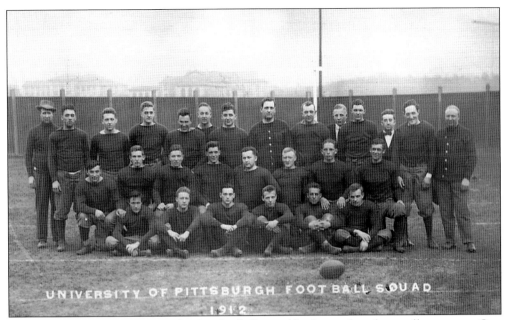

Before the days of Pop Warner, the Pitt football squad had some less-than-stellar seasons. One such campaign was in 1912, when the team, led by coach Joseph H. Thompson, after starting out 2-0 to finish with a 3-6 mark, lost six of its final seven contests, including a 38-0 thrashing by rival Penn State. (Courtesy of the University of Pittsburgh.)

Three years after the 1912 debacle, the Panthers won the first of nine national championships in 1915, as Warner, in his first season at the helm, led the club to an 8-0 record. Warner went on to win his first 30 games and three championships in four seasons, delighting Forbes Field crowds. (Courtesy of the University of Pittsburgh.)

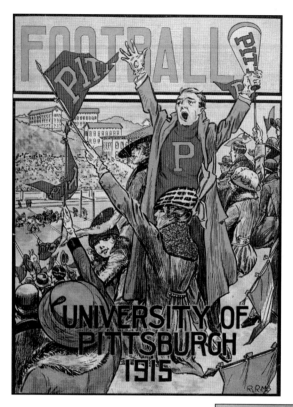

Pictured is a game program that was sold by the University of Pittsburgh at Forbes Field in 1915. The Panthers went 8-0 that season, winning their first national championship led by back Andy Hastings, who ran for 503 yards. The highlight was season-ending shutout victories against Carnegie Tech and Penn State at Forbes. (Courtesy of the University of Pittsburgh.)

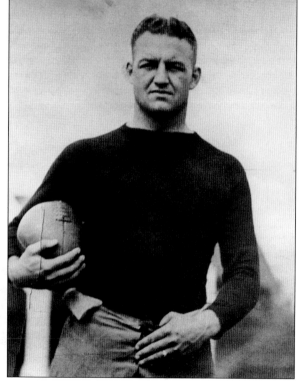

Center Herb Stein was selected as a consensus All-American in both 1920 and 1921. Also the captain of the 1920 club, Stein was considered one of the finest centers in the history of college football and was honored with his enshrinement in the College Football Hall of Fame in 1967. (Courtesy of the University of Pittsburgh.)

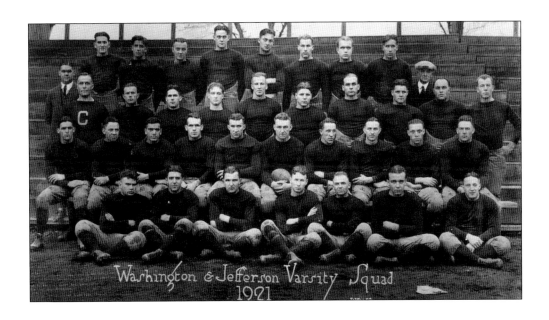

One of the Panthers biggest rivals in the 1910s and 1920s were the Washington and Jefferson Presidents. In 1921, Washington and Jefferson defeated the Panthers 7-0 at Forbes Field on their way to the Rose Bowl. In one of the most memorable Rose Bowls in the history of the annual event, they tied the heavily favored California Golden Bears 0-0 to complete their undefeated season at 10-0-1. The 1915 photograph below shows the game between the two rivals when Pitt defeated W & J 19-0. Overall, the two early rivals played each other until 1935, with the University of Pittsburgh winning the series 18-13-2. (Above, courtesy of Washington and Jefferson College; below, courtesy of Library of Congress, Prints and Photographs Division, LC-USZ62-127596.)

lead Grays,
ms of Homestead
icinity, 1913.

Formed in 1912, the Homestead Grays became one of the most legendary Negro League teams in the history of the sport. Pictured is the 1913 club which played as an independent team until 1929, when it moved to the American Negro League. It was that season that the Grays decided to call Forbes Field their home, where they won 11 league titles and three Negro World Series championships. The franchise stayed in Forbes until its demise in 1950. In 1940, the team used Griffith Stadium in Washington, DC, as a secondary home park, eventually playing two out of three of its games there in the mid-1940s, taking advantage of the increased attendance at Griffith.

During the early years of Forbes Field, fans were permitted to sit in the outfield to accommodate the overflow crowd when needed, a common practice during the time period. Ahead are the left field bleachers. The unlucky fans that sat in the upper corner of the bleachers could not see home plate because of the third base grandstand. Another unique fact about the facility was that beer was not permitted to be sold in the stadium, but fans were permitted to bring their own into the facility until 1960, when it was prohibited altogether. Fans would sometimes buy a second seat so they had a place for their beer. (Courtesy of Library of Congress, Prints and Photographs Division, LC-D4-15634 L.)

The star of the 1909 World Series, Babe Adams became one of the premiere control pitchers during his career. The 19-year veteran permitted only 1.29 bases on ball per nine innings, the 18th-lowest mark in major-league history. He set a record in 1914 against the New York Giants at Forbes Field, not allowing a walk over 21 innings.

Hugo Bezdek holds a unique distinction in the history of American sports as he was the only man ever to manage a major-league baseball team and coach both a major college football team as well as in the NFL. A college football Hall of Famer as well as a coach for the NFL's Cleveland Rams, Bezdek patrolled the dugout at Forbes Field as manager of the Bucs between 1917 and 1919.

In the 61-year history of Forbes Field, there was perhaps no better defensive player to patrol its vast center field than Max Carey. The speed that made him great defensively also made him a threat on the base paths as he swiped 738 bases over the course of his career, the ninth-best amount in the history of the game. He was elected to the Hall of Fame in 1961.

There was arguably no better left-hander in the history of the Pittsburgh Pirates than Wilbur Cooper. The West Virginia native was a hurler with an effortless motion who racked up 202 wins over the course of his career for the Pirates. A winner of 20 games four times in his Pirate career, Cooper's 202 victories remains the franchise record to this day.

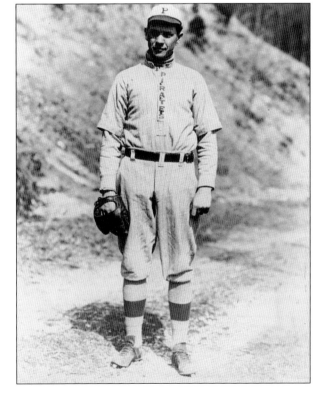

Breaking in with the Pirates in 1921 was catcher Johnny Gooch. Born in Smyrna, Tennessee, Gooch was a very efficient defensive catcher who had a short temper and was suspended for a short time in 1924 for using improper language toward an umpire. Gooch played in two World Series for the Bucs, in 1925 and 1927, and was traded to Brooklyn in 1928.

One of baseball's first Bonus Baby's, Marty O'Toole was signed by Barney Dreyfuss in 1911. O'Toole had an impressive minor league career and was the target of a bidding war by no less than seven major-league clubs. Dreyfuss outbid them all, paying the then unheard-of price of $22,500 for the hurler. O'Toole was not worth the money, winning only 27 times in his major-league career.

One of the first major-league hurlers to wear glasses, Lee "Specs" Meadows thrilled Forbes Field crowds for seven seasons. Toiling in the majors for eight years, Meadows came to the Bucs in 1923 and enjoyed his greatest successes, leading Pittsburgh to two National League pennants and winning 20 games in 1926.

A Hall of Famer who won 270 games over a 19-year career, Burleigh Grimes came to Pittsburgh in 1928 in a trade with the Giants for Vic Aldridge. The last legal spitballer in baseball history, Grimes won 25 games in his first season at Forbes Field and 17 his next before the Bucs dealt him to Boston.

Standing to the left of Pres. Warren Harding (center) and New York Yankees pitcher Bullet Joe Bush is Washington Senators legendary pitcher Walter Johnson. Winner of 417 major-league games, second-most in the history of the sport, Johnson was 37 years old and towards the end of his magnificent career when he faced the Pittsburgh Pirates in the 1925 World Series. After dominating the Bucs in games one and four, giving up only one run, the Hall of Fame hurler was battered by Pittsburgh in the rain at Forbes Field in game seven, surrendering nine runs and 15 hits in the 9-7 loss. (Courtesy of Library of Congress, Prints and Photographs Division, LC-DIG-ggbain-35843.)

Leading the Pittsburgh Pirates back up the ladder to the top of the National League in the mid- to late 1920s were three Hall of Fame players. Pictured above is Harold "Pie" Traynor, who joined the club in 1922. One of the greatest third baseman in the history of the game, Traynor hit .320 in 1925 as he helped the Bucs win the World Series. Left is the only brother combination in major-league history to be elected to the Hall of Fame, Lloyd (left) and Paul Waner. Together for the first time in 1927, the three powered the Bucs to the National League pennant, with Paul leading the league with a .380 average and 131 RBIs, Lloyd hitting .355 in his rookie campaign, and Pie chipping in with a .342 average.

Hitting .294 in 1925 for the defending world champion Washington Senators was shortstop Roger Peckinpaugh. Shown sliding in safely for his only stolen base of the 1925 World Series, this photograph is one of the few highlights Peckinpaugh had in the ill-fated series. He went on to make eight errors in the series that the Bucs won in seven games. (Courtesy of Library of Congress, Prints and Photographs Division, LC-USZ62-135444.)

Tagged out at second base on a failed hit-and-run by Pittsburgh shortstop Glenn Wright is Senators first baseman Joe Judge. After hitting .385 in the 1924 series, Judge had a poor 1925 Fall Classic against the Pirates, with a paltry .174 mark, although he did hit his only World Series homer with a long ball in the opener. (Courtesy of Library of Congress, Prints and Photographs Division, LC-USZ62-135448.)

Ray Kremer got a late start in his major-league career, but certainly made the most of his opportunity. A 31-year-old rookie in 1924, Kremer lit up the league with 18 wins and a league high of four shutouts. He went on to lead the Bucs to two National League pennants, winning 20 games twice and also captured the league ERA crown in 1926 and 1927.

Pictured left is Pirates Hall of Fame center fielder Max Carey stealing a base in game four of the 1925 World Series. A .285 career hitter, Carey was at his best in his only World Series appearance. Carey made the most of his lone post-season, hitting .458 in the seven-game series with four doubles and eleven hits. (Courtesy of Library of Congress, Prints and Photographs Division, LC-USZ62-135446.)

Pictured are the managers who led the Pirates to their first two World Series championships, Fred Clarke (right) and Bill McKechnie (below). The two Hall of Famers became linked together in Pirate lore for one of the most embarrassing moments in team history. In 1926, the two became the center of a controversy, as Clarke, by then a bench coach as well as the director of scouting, suggested to McKechnie, the manager, that he pull Max Carey out of the lineup and replace him with anyone. Upon hearing of the comment, Carey along with Babe Adams and Carson Bigbee complained to Barney Dreyfuss, asking for Clarke to be removed from the bench. The three players were dropped from the team, and the controversy cost McKechnie his job at the end of the season.

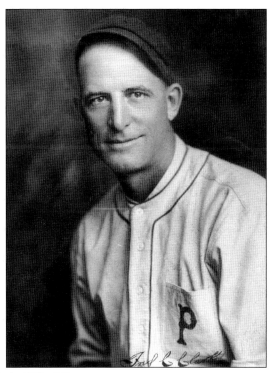

Coming over from the Chicago Cubs in a trade before the 1925 campaign, first baseman George Grantham seemed to be just what the Pirates needed. He hit .326 in the Bucs world championship campaign, but was not a factor in the series, hitting only .133. Two years later, while Pittsburgh lost the series in 1927, Grantham was much more effective in that Fall Classic, with a .364 mark.

Other than Bill Mazeroski's home run in game seven of the 1960 World Series, the greatest moment the history of Forbes Field had was the eighth inning of the seventh game in the 1925 World Series. Led by a two-out, two-run double by Kiki Cuyler (pictured), Pittsburgh scored three runs to erase a one-run deficit on the way to a 9-7 win and the world championship.

Pitchers Carmen Hill (left) and Lee Meadows (right), not only shared the fact that they were two of the very few players in major-league history to wear glasses during that time period, but that they were two very important members of the 1927 National League champion Pirates. Meadows finished the season 19-10, while Hill did him one better, with a team high of 22 wins.

Between 1922 and 1924, middle infielder Rabbit Maranville (left) and manager Bill McKechnie teamed up to help the Pirates climb back into the first division of the National League standings. In the three years they were together, Pittsburgh finished in third place each season. Maranville was dealt to the Cubs after the 1924 campaign, a year before the Bucs won a world championship.

In the long history of the Pittsburgh Pirates, there have been very few players who could even be held in the same breath as Paul "Glee" Waner. A pitcher for East Central State Teachers College ,where he was 23-4, Waner began his minor league career as a pitcher until former Pirate Dots Miller, his manager in San Francisco, moved him to the outfield after Waner developed a sore arm. The move proved very fortuitous. He broke in with the Bucs in 1926 with a .336 average and never looked back. He hit well over .300 for his first 12 seasons and finished his 20-year major-league career with a .333 mark and 3,152 hits.

According to Paul Waner in the renowned book by Lawrence Ritter *The Glory of their Times*, Clyde Barnhart was a "butterball" weighing 260 to 270 pounds in one of his early spring trainings. He eventually took the weight off and became a pivotal part of the two championship Pirate squads in the 1920s, hitting .325 in 1925 and .319 two years later.

A fine shortstop with the Detroit Tigers in the early part of the 20th century, Donie Bush came to Pittsburgh in 1927, following the controversial dismissal of manager Bill McKechnie in 1926. The Pirate faithful that came through the turnstiles at Forbes Field in 1927 quickly forgot about the issues of the season before, as Bush led the club to the National League pennant.

45

As a 20-year-old, shortstop Dick Bartell broke in with the Pittsburgh Pirates in 1928, hitting .305 in 72 games. His star shined even brighter two years later when he hit .320. The problem was that Bartell often argued with Pirate president Barney Dreyfuss, who was not always easy to deal with. The fiery relationship led to Bartell being traded to the Phillies after 1930 despite his excellent season.

Playing sporadically for the Pittsburgh Pirates in the early 1920s, Jewel Winklemeyer Ens finally returned in 1929 as a manager for the team. Ens took over from Donie Bush, whom he replaced with 35 games left in the season. Ens led the Bucs to a 21-14 mark that season and stayed with the club for two seasons before being let go after a 75-79 mark in 1931.

Three

1931–1950
More than Just Baseball

Not even two miles separate the three major universities in Pittsburgh. Drive down Forbes Avenue, starting near the old jail, past Duquesne University; a little further up the road is the University of Pittsburgh; a couple blocks farther is Carnegie Mellon University, or Carnegie Tech, as it was known on the first half of the 20th century.

These three universities are renowned for their academics for sure, but in the 1930s through the early 1940s, they were major players in the college football world, as many college football aficionados would descend on the Oakland area of the city to see these teams perform between Pitt Stadium and Forbes Field. All three schools would be ranked in the top 10 at one time or another, and they would all play in major bowls. Pitt won four national championships, while the Dukes were ranked number one in the Massey Ratings in 1941.

It was a different time for Forbes Field between 1930 and 1950. Except for a few years in the mid- to late 1930s, the Pirates were rarely in contention, so the fans who entered Forbes turned towards college football as well as boxing, and some of the greatest pugilists ever to lace up the gloves not only came from the area but fought in this fabulous facility.

The decrepit Steelers even played their lone postseason contest at Forbes in 1947, an ill-fated game that saw them lose the Eastern Division championship to Philadelphia.

While baseball was still the primary tenant, it was during this time that Forbes Field gave fans many special memories of the sports world as a whole. It may not have been the best of times for the Pirates, but it was indeed the golden era for this treasured stadium.

While the majority of its 61-year existence saw Forbes Field play host mostly to baseball, for most of the first half of its tenure it doubled as the home to the best football Pittsburgh had to offer. The University of Pittsburgh team won three national championships while calling Forbes its home, and Duquesne University became a national power in the mid-1930s and early 1940s. The Pittsburgh Steelers played at Forbes Field for the first 30 seasons of its existence, between 1933 and 1963. Through it all, perhaps the greatest football game ever to be played within these walls was in 1926, when Carnegie Tech faced off against Notre Dame. Having been outscored 111-19 the previous four seasons, Tech surprised the Fighting Irish, beating them 19-0. ESPN has called the game one of the greatest upsets in the history of the sport.

Perhaps the greatest player ever to don a uniform for the Duquesne University Dukes was center Mike Basrak. Basrak had a phenomenal 1936 campaign, leading the Dukes to a 7-2-0 season and a spot in the Orange Bowl. For his efforts, Basrak was named a first team All-American, the first player to be accorded such an honor in school history. (Courtesy of Duquesne University.)

In 1936, Duquesne University hit the big time in college football as the squad, led by coach John "Clipper" Smith, finished with a 7-2-0 mark that included victories over both their city counterparts, Pitt and Carnegie Tech. They went on to defeat Mississippi State in the Orange Bowl 13-12 and finished the season ranked 14th by the Associated Press. (Courtesy of Duquesne University.)

One of Notre Dame's famed "Four Horsemen," Elmer Layden became coach at Duquesne in 1927. While there, he not only made his mark on the city's football history by playing Pittsburgh's first night football game against Geneva at Forbes Field in 1929, but led the team to a spot in the Festival of Palms game in 1933, a 33-7 win over Miami (Florida). (Courtesy of Duquesne University.)

With time running out in the 1937 Orange Bowl and the Duquesne Dukes down 12-7 against the underdog Mississippi State Bulldogs, halfback Boyd Brumbaugh heaved a desperate pass from his own 28-yard line to Ernie Hefferle. Hefferle grabbed the toss and took it the remainder of the 72 yards, completing the greatest play in school history and a 13-12 Dukes win. (Courtesy of Duquesne University.)

Aldo "Buff" Donelli (left) was one of the greatest soccer players in United States history and also took Duquesne football to the highest level in the program's history. A member of the USA National team in the World Cup in 1934, Donelli scored all four goals in the United States' 4-1 qualifying victory against Mexico. He was named to the National Soccer Hall of Fame, but it was his time on the Dukes sideline that he is most noted for in Pittsburgh. Taking over in 1939, he led the Dukes to a 29-4-1 mark in four seasons, including a number 10 ranking in 1939 and a number eight ranking two years later, when his defense only gave up 21 points in nine games. Decades later, when calculating national champions of the past, the Massey Rankings computer dubbed the Dukes as national champions in 1941. The man at right is unidentified. (Courtesy of Duquesne University.)

CRAWFORDS of 1932
3-18-32

Pictured are the 1932 Pittsburgh Crawfords. While they played their games in a stadium built specifically for them, Greenlee Field, named after their owner Gus Greenlee, they spent time at Forbes Field playing the Homestead Grays. The Crawfords raided the Grays for several of their best players, including Josh Gibson, and their 1935 squad is considered among the best in Negro League history.

One of the most sure-handed defensive third baseman in Negro League history, Judy Johnson was also an effective .300 hitter. He patrolled the Forbes Field infield for the Homestead Grays in 1930 and 1937, but was more known for his spectacular play with the Crawfords in between his seasons with the Grays. Johnson was elected to the Baseball Hall of Fame in 1975.

He is celebrated as the greatest power hitter the Negro Leagues ever knew, and if the eyewitness accounts of those who actually saw him play are to be believed, perhaps the greatest in baseball history—Josh Gibson. Born in Georgia but growing up in Pittsburgh, Gibson was able to dazzle his hometown fans for both the Homestead Grays and Pittsburgh Crawfords. So great was his power that he is the only player ever to hit a ball out of Yankee Stadium. As amazing a hitter as he was, he was equally adept defensively as a catcher. Unfortunately, while he was playing when the major leagues integrated, he was not signed and died of a stroke in 1947 at age 35.

Combining with Josh Gibson to give the Homestead Grays a devastating one-two power combination, Buck Leonard was one of the most complete hitters in Negro League history. Unlike Gibson, Leonard stuck with the Grays for 17 seasons, hitting .320 while being a slick, defensive first baseman. He was elected to the Hall of Fame in 1972.

There was no faster man in the Negro Leagues than James "Cool Papa" Bell. A winner of the Triple Crown in the Mexican League in 1940, Bell brought his incredible talent to Pittsburgh, playing with the Grays first in 1932, then between 1943 and 1946, as well as the Crawfords from 1933 to 1937. He finished his 21-year career in 1946 with a .317 average.

The Great Dizzy Dean once said, "Charleston could hit that ball a mile. He didn't have a weakness." A .351 hitter over the course of his 26-year Negro League career, Oscar Charleston graced the infield at Forbes Field with the Grays in 1930 and 1931, before signing with the legendary crosstown Crawfords.

Smokey Joe Williams was a dominant pitcher when the Negro Leagues were in their infancy. But it was not until later on that he found his way to Pittsburgh, signing with the Grays in 1925. When Homestead joined the Negro American League in 1929, Williams was 44-years-old yet finished second in winning percentage. In 1999, he was recognized for his career when he was elected to the Baseball Hall of Fame.

A member of the Pro and College Football Hall of Fame, as well as an outfielder with the Cincinnati Reds, Greasy Neale came to Pittsburgh at a time when professional football in the city was at a low point. In 1943, when the Eagles and Steelers combined to form the Steagles, he was co-coach and combatant with Walt Kiesling. Despite the issues, Neale helped guide the Steagles to a 5-4-1 mark. (Courtesy of Library of Congress, Prints and Photographs Division, LC-B2- 4992-14.)

After a 15-year career at the Pitt, where he won five national championships, Jock Sutherland was hired to coach the Pittsburgh Steelers in 1946. A year later, he led them to a first place tie with the Eagles, and they faced off at Forbes for a one-game playoff. Pittsburgh lost 21-0 in their lone postseason game until 1972. Sutherland tragically died a year later. (Courtesy of the University of Pittsburgh.)

Arguably the greatest boxer in Pittsburgh history, light heavyweight Billy Conn was more famous for his two losses for the heavyweight championship to Joe Louis than he was for his fabulous career; but make no mistake, it was fabulous. He finished with a 63-11-1 mark, many bouts coming within the walls of Forbes Field in a 14-year career, and won the light heavyweight championship of the world in 1939, defeating Melio Bettina. Before battling Louis, Conn successfully defended his belt three times. He was elected to the Boxing Hall of Fame in 1965; and in 2000, the Associated Press named him one of the top 10 fighters of the 20th century. (Both, courtesy of Timothy Conn.)

Two of Pittsburgh's greatest boxers, Billy Conn (left) and Fritzie Zivic (right), share a laugh together in this photograph. The Croat Comet, as Zivic was called, fought many times at Forbes Field. His first bout there came on July 30, 1936, on the same card with Conn, who also made his Forbes debut that night. Zivic beat Laddie Tonielli with a six-round TKO. (Courtesy of Timothy Conn.)

Of the many events that took place at Forbes Field outside of its main purpose—housing the Pittsburgh Pirates—concerts were some of the most popular. Pictured here is a musical event that featured many groups, bands, and choirs that entertained the many music enthusiasts in the city during the time period.

Facing the ivy-less wall at Forbes Field, the Pirates and their opponents respectfully listen to the national anthem played by a local band. One of the most bittersweet seasons for the Pirates occurred in 1938, when for the better part of the campaign, Pittsburgh thrilled Pirate fans at Forbes Field, looking like the team was on the precipice of winning its seventh National League pennant. Pittsburgh had a seven-game lead on the Chicago Cubs on September 4, but when the Pirates met Chicago on September 28, the lead had all but slipped away. They lost to the Cubs that day 6-5 on a Gabby Hartnett home run—losing their lead and eventually the pennant a few days later.

In the 61-year history of Forbes Field, there were many changes and much work that went on during the off-season to keep Pittsburghers feeling proud. Pictured above is the stadium following the 1946 campaign, when a couple cosmetic changes occurred. The first was the press box, which was lowered a level, and the addition of more field boxes for the fans. The photograph below shows the stadium after the 1948 Steeler campaign when GM Roy Hamey (left) and assistant treasurer Al Schlensker (right) overlook a pile of dirt that is intended to correct a 15-inch sinkage in left field and a minor one in center field.

A group of ladies cheers on the Pittsburgh Pirates at Forbes Field in the 1940s. Ladies Day was a tradition in baseball in the late 19th century and a good part of the 20th. On June 16, 1883, the New York Giants had the first Ladies Day, admitting women free of charge. The tradition continued at Forbes, as many women wildly cheered on the Bucs over the years.

A backup shortstop for the Pirates in 1944, Frankie Zak was one of the most quizzical picks to an All-Star game. The game was played at Forbes Field and when the original pick, Eddie Miller, had to bow out due to an injury, Zak was picked as the replacement since he was already in the city. The National League won the game 7-1 in front of 29,589 patrons at Forbes.

Parading around Forbes Field in the "official" car of the Pirates station, KDKA-TV, is announcer Rosey Rowswell. Rowswell had a 19-year career broadcasting Pirate games and was one of the first unabashed "homers," rooting openly for the Bucs during his broadcasts. The frail, 110-pound Rowswell retired in 1955, turning the mike over to another legend, Bob Prince.

The Pirates line up down the first base line as a packed Forbes Field honors the nation during the national anthem. Over the years at Forbes Field, many changes were made, including in 1938, when an extra level was built behind home plate called the Crow's Nest in anticipation of the 1938 World Series. The Pirates never made it, as they blew a seven-game lead in September.

Pictured here, Pirate first baseman Elbie Fletcher smacked a 425-foot three-run homer in the first inning during an 8-2 defeat of the Brooklyn Dodgers in 1943. Fletcher came to the Pirates from the Boston Braves in 1939 and hit .279 with 60 home runs in his seven years in a Pirate uniform.

Lined up in the Forbes Field dugout are four members of the 1942 Pittsburgh Pirates. From left to right are outfielder Vince DiMaggio, catcher Babe Phelps, first baseman Elbie Fletcher, and third baseman Bob Elliott. Coming off a successful 1941, the crew struggled in 1942, finishing 66-81 while hitting a meager .245 as a team.

He was coming to the end of his epic career when Babe Ruth and the Boston Braves met the Pittsburgh Pirates at Forbes Field on May 25, 1935. With Ruth having a horrendous season, trying to hang on hoping the Braves would offer him a chance to be the manager down the road, no one expected to see what was arguably the greatest regular season moment in the history of Forbes Field. Ruth went on to hit three home runs that day, the final one being the first ever to clear the right field roof. They were the last three of his career, as he retired for good five days later. (Courtesy of Library of Congress, Prints and Photographs Division, LC-B2-5463-14.)

One of the greatest offensive shortstops was Floyd "Arky" Vaughan. A Pirate for 10 seasons, Vaughan hit .318 for his career, including a magnificent .385 in 1935 that not only set the franchise record, which he still holds to this day, but is the highest a shortstop hit in the 20th century. Dying in a tragic drowning accident in 1952, Vaughan was elected to the Hall of Fame in 1985.

The only shortstop who was better than Arky Vaughan in Pittsburgh Pirate history was one of the greatest in the history of the game, Honus Wagner. A .328 lifetime hitter, Wagner became a coach with the club in 1933, remaining there for 19 seasons. While he never wore a number during his playing career, 33, which he wore as a coach, was retired in 1952. Wagner died in 1955.

After the death of Barney Dreyfuss, his son-in-law Bill Benswanger took over as club president. Benswanger, a pianist who was also director of the Pittsburgh Symphony Orchestra for 20 years, was chosen to run the club because he was the only male in the family. The team never won a World Series in his 15-season tenure, which ended when he sold the club to the Galbreath family in 1946.

Better known as the manager of the Pittsburgh Pirates who led them to world championships in 1960 and 1971, Danny Murtaugh also played for the club in the late 1940s, between 1948 and 1951. A second baseman for the team, Murtaugh had his most effective seasons in 1948 and 1950 when he hit .290 and .294, respectively.

In the summer of 1949, Forbes Field fans were thrilled by the exploits of baseball's next superstar, Dino Restelli. In his second major-league game that season, he hit two home runs and drove in five. Restelli hit 12 homers and drove in 40 in only 72 games his rookie season. His star would fade as quickly as it came, and he was out of the majors by 1952.

Waiting to congratulate Bob Elliott (crossing home plate) after a home run is Vince DiMaggio (No. 9). The brother of the more famous Joe DiMaggio, Vince was solid if unspectacular for the Pirates in his five seasons in Pittsburgh during World War II. He hit .255 with 79 home runs during that time period.

While 12-year veteran Debs Garms only spent two seasons in Pittsburgh, his short tenure was more than productive. In 1940, Garms hit .355 in only 385 at bats to capture the National League batting title. Because he had so few at bats, it eventually prompted league officials to change the rules to first 400 at bats and then 3.1 at bats per game to qualify for a title.

A large crowd lines up to enter Forbes Field at the Sennott Street entrance before a game in 1948. In an era that was one of the worst in the history of the franchise—between 1946 and 1958—1948 was the lone bright spot. Some 1,517,021 fans jammed Forbes to see the surprising Pirates, led by Ralph Kiner who had 40 homers and 123 RBIs, finish 83-71.

Taking over for Pie Traynor in 1940 was the former St. Louis Cardinal great Frankie "The Fordham Flash" Frisch (center). Winning a World Series with the Cardinals in 1934 as well as guiding St. Louis to two second-place finishes, Frisch was unable to manage the Pirates to a pennant. His best year was in 1944 when Pittsburgh was 90-63. He was released during the 1946 campaign.

As classy an individual as ever stepped on the diamond at Forbes Field, Gus Suhr was a staple for the Pirates at first base between 1930 and 1939. Other than a solid .279 average, the major thing he was known for as a Pirate was playing in a then National League record 822 games. When he died in 2004, he was the oldest living Pirate at 98 years.

To entice one of the greatest power hitters the game had known to come to Pittsburgh, new Pirate owner John Galbreath not only made the veteran slugger Hank Greenberg the first $100,000 player in baseball, but promised to build a bull pen in left field that made the cavernous Forbes Field a little easier place to hit a home run in. The new bullpen area would be called "Greenberg Gardens." Greenberg spent one season with the Bucs, not only hitting 23 home runs, but more importantly becoming the mentor to Ralph Kiner, helping the young Pirate power hitter become one of the best in the game himself, winning a still major-league record seven consecutive home run titles.

Four

1951–1959
THE BASEMENT

Before the 1960s, when it seemed like a good idea to build ballparks in cement wastelands where parking was ample and walking to the ballpark was tantamount to a Donner Party excursion, ballparks were built in cities.

In Pittsburgh, Forbes Field was built in what could be called Pittsburgh's "second city"— Oakland. Located at the widening end of the triangle and separated from downtown by a number of neighborhoods, Oakland meant parks and the University of Pittsburgh.

And while today Pitt has grown and spread along with a handful of other colleges, including Carnegie Mellon University, the symbol that identifies the area is the Cathedral of Learning.

Until the end of the 1960s, below the cathedral was Forbes Field, which after so many years of hosting champions and championships in both football and baseball, presided in the 1950s over some of the worst teams the Steel City has ever seen.

Following the tumultuous war years, Columbus, Ohio, native John Galbreath bought the Pirates, and while he eventually would enjoy incredible success on the diamond, in the late 1940s and early to mid-1950s, the Pirates were nothing more than Ralph Kiner and a collection of castoffs that stood at the bottom of the National League standings more times than not, a position that they often shared with the Steelers, who also produced less-than-stellar clubs during the time period.

While the Steelers remained poor, the Pirates began to add a collection of young talent that began to dig themselves out of the doldrums setting up a championship in 1960 that remains among the most memorable Forbes Field had ever seen.

The University of Pittsburgh's Cathedral of Learning, situated nearby, provides a dramatic backdrop to Forbes Field as it seems to rise from just behind the mid-left field foul line and seats beyond. Dedicated in 1937, it is currently the tallest educational building in the United States. (Courtesy of David Finoli.)

On the night of April 28, 1955, the Pittsburgh Pirates take on the Cincinnati Reds at Forbes Field. The sparse Forbes crowd of 6,907 thought the Pirates had a victory all but secured until Reds third baseman Ray Jablonski crushed a two-run double off of Pirate starter Dick Littlefield to give Cincinnati a 3-2 win.

Before multiuse facilities were invented, ballparks of the era served the purpose. Here, Forbes Field hosts a college football game between Duquesne and St. Louis in 1949, a game the Dukes won 51-14. Note in the photograph below that the Forbes Field batting cages are put off to the side of the stadium so it could comfortably host the game. While Duquesne University was a big part of the tradition with its excellent squads in the late 1930s and early 1940s, by the 1950s, the magic had ended as Duquesne was unable to continue it excellence, eventually necessitating the school to drop football after the 1950 campaign. (Courtesy of Duquesne University.)

The name of Pittsburgh Steelers' owner Art Rooney spans the city. But before the lowly Steelers rated their own home on Pittsburgh's North Side, they played at Forbes Field. This statue of the iconic owner sits near Gate D of Heinz Field and celebrates all the success he led the Steelers to over the years. That success was not very evident in the 1950s. While it was not the worst decade in team history, the Steelers nonetheless were mired in mediocrity, struggling for the most part around the .500 level or below until they finished 7-4-1 in 1958. (Courtesy of David Finoli.)

Pirate general manager Branch Rickey is sitting third from left in the photograph above and is seated speaking to his team at spring training in the early 1950s in the photograph below. Rickey, who started his career as a player with the St. Louis Browns and New York Highlanders in the early part of the 20th century and later on managed the Browns, became a Hall of Famer as the legendary general manager of St. Louis Cardinals between 1919 and 1942, when he instituted the farm system, and then with the Brooklyn Dodgers, when he broke the racial barrier, signing Jackie Robinson in 1945. Rickey came to the Bucs in 1950 and began to put together the pieces of their 1960 World Championship, signing such notable players as Roberto Clemente, Bill Mazeroski, and Bob Friend.

Two Baseball Hall of Famers, Pittsburgh Pirates Ralph Kiner and New York Giants Johnny Mize, pose before a game at Forbes Field. Two of the preeminent sluggers of their day, Mize and Kiner were in a titanic struggle for the home run title in 1947 and 1948, tying each year for the National League crown.

During his career, Ralph Kiner established himself as a power hitter. The left center field porch at Forbes Field was named "Kiner's Korner" for the home runs he deposited there. He led the National League in home runs for seven consecutive seasons, ending with his 37-home-runs season in 1952. Despite the team's bad records, Kiner drew many fans to Forbes Field, just to see him bat.

Joe Garagiola did not have a successful career as a catcher in the majors, but he went on to become a great broadcaster. The one-time catcher for the Cubs, Giants, Pirates, and Cardinals went on to greater fame as a play-by-play announcer for many nationally televised baseball games in the 1960s, 1970s, and 1980s. Here, he is pictured in a dugout at Forbes Field.

Vic Janowicz was a tragic figure in baseball. After a Heisman Trophy career at Ohio State, Janowicz passed up professional football for baseball. He spent two seasons with Pittsburgh, hitting .214. Janowicz left baseball and signed with the Washington Redskins. In 1956, he suffered brain injuries in an automobile accident. His name can be found in his hometown of Elyria, Ohio, with a baseball field and street named after the former Heisman Trophy winner to honor his athletic success.

John Beradino found his life's work in front of a camera rather than turning double plays. *General Hospital*'s Dr. Steve Hardy was an infielder who finished his career in Pittsburgh's Forbes Field after a leg injury in 1952. Along with his time on *General Hospital*, Beradino acted with Frank Sinatra and with Cary Grant in Alfred Hitchcock's *North by Northwest.*

One can change the game all he wants, but long before the start of the game, kids and autograph-seekers will line the field seats' rail looking for attention from their favorite players. Here, fans line the rail down the third base line at Forbes Field hoping to see and chat with their favorite players.

Cliff Chambers pitched for the Pittsburgh Pirates in the early 1950s. A nondescript major leaguer with a 48-53 career mark made history on May 6, 1951, in the second game of a doubleheader at Braves Field in Boston, when Chambers came off a sickbed to pitch a no-hitter, beating the Boston Braves.

Presenting the colors for the national anthem in a game in the late 1950s are members of the armed forces. During the 1958 campaign, fans came back to Forbes Field in droves as the young Pirates finally were back in contention for the pennant after a decade of losing. 1,311,908 fans came through the turnstiles to see Pittsburgh finish in second place, an increase of almost half a million over 1957.

Forbes Field was stuck in the middle of the Oakland neighborhood and the University of Pittsburgh campus. Trolley cars, jammed parking, and city neighborhoods filled the park. A more affluent area of Pittsburgh at the turn of the 20th century, which is one of the reasons Pirate president Barney Dreyfuss moved his team from Exposition Park on the North Side of the city to Forbes Field, today Oakland has not only become one of the educational center of Pittsburgh—with Pitt, Carnegie Mellon and Carlow University—but a hub in the medical community, with UPMC medical facilities, as well as home to many important cultural facilities.

It is not just the players on the field that makes the game; it is the folks in the stand who keep the fans fed and happy. At Forbes Field, head of concessions Myron O'Brisky (left) organized the people who kept those baseball fans happy. He is pictured next to manager Billy Meyer, who led the Bucs to a surprise 83-71 mark in 1948.

Gene Mauch, who made his professional reputation as a major-league manager from 1960 through 1987, spent 1947 looking after second base as a reserve at Forbes Field for the Pittsburgh Pirates. While never making much of a mark as a player, Mauch did play in parts of nine major-league seasons for six teams, hitting .239.

If Roberto Clemente made right field at Forbes Field his own, it was Howard Frederick "Howie" Haak that put him there. The pioneer of baseball scouting in Latin America is responsible for finding and signing many of the players that made the Pirates' championships in the 1970s possible, including his part in the Pirates drafting Clemente from the Dodger farm system in the 1954 Rule V draft.

William Mazeroski dominated territory around Forbes Field's second base, providing sure-handed defense, and was part of a shutdown double play. At bat, he sprayed hits all over Forbes Field as one of the best offensive second baseman in the National League in the 1960s, securing the starting spot at second in 1957 until injuries began to take their toll in 1968.

Singer, actor, baseball club owner, Bing Crosby was a minority owner of the Pirates beginning in 1946, when the Barney Dreyfuss family was replaced by a group headed by Frank McKinney. Crosby made occasional appearances at Forbes Field and participated in radio broadcasts now and then. The late Crosby recently made the news again when it was discovered he had what was the only tape of game seven of the 1960 World Series.

While most Pittsburghers of a certain age will remember Paul Long as a WTAE-TV newscaster, from 1957 through 1962 he joined legendary Pirates broadcaster Bob Prince in the booth at Forbes Field. Long, who was an anchor for the WTAE news in Pittsburgh from 1969 to 1994, died in 2002 at the age of 86.

While it had become one of the iconic sights at the University of Pittsburgh, the Cathedral of Learning also was one of the dominant sights at Forbes Field. Looking out over the bleachers down the third base line, Pirate fans enjoyed a breathtaking view of the building that houses many offices and classrooms for the university's liberal arts schools.

Modern stadiums get spectators in and out pretty quickly, but when fans are having a season like the 1960 Pittsburgh Pirates, even PNC Park could not do any better than old Forbes Field could. Here, fans stand in the rain to pick up tickets for a game they hope will happen. That is a special season.

From right-center field seats, one can see Oakland peaking above the top deck and press boxes for Forbes Field, and Schenley Park is behind the outfield wall. The capacity at Forbes Field went through a lot of changes over its history, beginning at 23,000 seats, increasing to 41,000 from 1925 to 1937, declining to 33,467 in the mid-1940s, and settling to 35,000 until it closed in 1970.

Robert Del Greco was a fast, defensively sound outfielder for Pittsburgh before being traded to the Cardinals for Bill Virdon in 1956. In 1957, the Yankees acquired him to fill in for Mickey Mantle in the late innings. Following his retirement, Del Greco went to work as a driver for *The Pittsburgh Press* and threw batting practice for the Pirates until the early 1990s. His son is a highly regarded attorney.

Elroy Face helped invent the job of closer for major-league baseball teams. Pictured is Face throwing his legendary forkball. After his record setting 18-1 mark in 1959, Face set another record in the 1960 World Series against the New York Yankees, becoming the first pitcher to save three games in a series.

As the 1950s moved to the 1960s, no Pirates pitcher dominated Forbes Field like Bob Friend. From 1951 to 1962, Friend was a four time all-star despite having a losing career record with a 191-218 mark. He won the National League ERA crown in 1955 and pitched in the 1960 World Series.

Joe E. Brown was an actor and comedian who became a fixture at Forbes Field after his son Joe L. Brown became Pirates general manager in 1955. Brown Sr. had a lifelong love affair with baseball. He was offered a contract with the New York Yankees but decided acting was his vocation. From left to right are Bob Friend, Joe E. Brown, Dale Long, and Frank Thomas. During his impressive acting career, the comedian starred in many films—even landing the role of a baseball player, appearing as a Cardinal in the movie *Fireman, Save My Child*. Brown traveled extensively to entertain the troops during World War II and was one of only two civilians to be awarded the Bronze Star during the war.

Danny Murtaugh was a second baseman for the Pirates from 1948 to 1951, when his playing career ended after nine major-league seasons when he hit .254. He is best remembered, however, as the manager who led the Pirates to two World Series titles, including the thrilling 1960 World Series that ended in Forbes Field.

Managers Danny Murtaugh (left) and Bill McKechnie ran teams from the home dugout at Forbes Field. McKechnie, who was enshrined in the Hall of Fame in 1962, won National League pennants with three different teams, including the Pirates. The club's spring-training ballpark in Bradenton, Florida, is named for McKechnie.

Summertime 1958 in Oakland, Pittsburgh, Pennsylvania, is pictured as crowds line up to get into Forbes Field for a Pirates game during their surprise campaign. In 1958, the Pirates sold Forbes Field to the University of Pittsburgh, and it was anticipated the park would be closed soon thereafter to make way for expansion of the university.

The baseball experience extends far beyond the ballpark, and that has been the function of radio and eventually television. The atmosphere of the Pittsburgh Pirates of the 1950s and 1960s is inseparable from the power of KDKA radio's 50,000 watts of broadcasting power and the voice of Bob Prince. Here, KDKA hosts a "Teen Night" at Forbes Field.

In one of the stranger achievements on May 26, 1959, pitcher Harvey Haddix retired 36 consecutive Milwaukee Braves batters in 12 innings. It was arguably the greatest game ever pitched, but in a cruel twist of fate, the Pirates failed to score as an error in bottom of the 13th led to a 1-0 loss. The game was representative of an achievement that was never seen by Pirate fans at Forbes Field, as there were, surprisingly, no no-hitters ever pitched at the legendary facility, even though it was considered a pitchers' park. Despite the fact the game was an upsetting loss for Haddix, he came back pitching for the Pirates at Forbes Field until 1963 and was a pivotal part of their 1960 world championship squad, winning two contests in the World Series, including game seven.

Five

1960
WORLD CHAMPIONS

In every city that houses a major sports franchise, there is one season, one year, which is magical and will elicit memories and joy when it is brought up in a conversation. For the city of Pittsburgh, there have been many championships to choose from, but when speaking of that one special season, the topic begins and ends with the 1960 Pittsburgh Pirates.

Leading into that championship campaign, the Pirates had gone 35 years without winning a World Series; worse yet, from 1949 to 1957, they produced some of the worst teams in franchise history. Finally, in 1958, it looked like it was all coming together as young players like Roberto Clemente, Bill Mazeroski, Dick Groat, Vern Law, Bob Friend, and Elroy Face shocked the baseball world, finishing second to the Milwaukee Braves.

In the next two years, general manager Joe L. Brown had added such players as Don Hoak, Vinegar Bend Mizell, Harvey Haddix, and Smoky Burgess. It was the mix the team needed, as it ran to the National League pennant, defeating the Braves by seven games. The players' prize for their unexpected championship was to face the powerful New York Yankees, a team for which a World Series trip was an annual rite.

A then franchise record 1,705,828 Pirate faithful went through the turnstiles in 1960; for the Fall Classic, tickets were at a premium, as the two teams split the first six games—with Pittsburgh winning three close games and the Yankees emerging victorious in three one-sided contests.

On a sunny October 13 afternoon, 36,683 jammed Forbes Field to witness what not only would be one of the finest games in major-league history but also the greatest moment the legendary facility would ever see. The clubs battled back and forth as the Bucs went to bat in the bottom of the ninth with the score tied at nine. Mazeroski came up against New York's Ralph Terry and parked a pitch over the left field fence to conclude this fantasy campaign with the only home run to ever end a game seven in the World Series. The moment is immortalized today with a plaque outside of Posvar Hall on the campus of the University of Pittsburgh at the exact spot where the ball went over the fence, sending this town into a celebration that those who lived it will never forget.

John W. Galbreath made his fortune building skyscrapers in the United States and around the world. But he was also a sportsman; he used his fortune to invest in a successful racehorse stable and win the Kentucky Derby. From 1948 to 1985, he was the owner of the Pittsburgh Pirates. This period of Bucs history encompassed three of their modern-era World Series championships—in 1960, 1971, and 1979.

With owner Galbreath leading the business end of the team, he hired his chief lieutenant, general manager Joe L. Brown, son of comedian and actor Joe E. Brown, to run the on-the-field product. Brown was the lead talent spotter who made the Pittsburgh Pirates a premier club in the 1960s, slowly and surely bringing along the talent that not only won the 1960 World Series but also reloaded and dominated the 1970s.

Some players have long, illustrious careers; others come and go with little notice. Gino Cimoli was a player who found his moment at Forbes Field. In the eighth inning of the seventh game of the 1960 World Series, Cimoli slapped a pinch-hit single that started a five-run rally against the New York Yankees that gave the Bucs a temporary 9-7 lead.

Harvey Haddix will always be remembered for his perfect-game loss, but in 1960, he was a mainstay of the World Series champion Pirates. At Yankee Stadium, Haddix was dominating in a game-five win. Two games later, at Forbes Field, Haddix pitched in relief and earned the win on Bill Mazeroski's historic home run.

Forbes Field, now an elderly 51 years old, enjoyed its glory days in 1960. The improbable Pittsburgh Pirates enjoyed success that year as a franchise record 1,705,828 jammed the park and often flooded Oakland with baseball fans. This photograph shows of the left field seat on a sunny afternoon during a game against the Chicago Cubs.

Sublime Pittsburgh Pirate right fielder and hitter Roberto Clemente was just beginning to emerge as a great baseball player in the 1960s. His speed, glove, and powerful arm made right field in Forbes Field useless for opposing hitters. Clemente hit .314 that year, but finished a disappointing eighth in the 1960 MVP race, a slight that reportedly prompted Clemente to never wear his ring from that season.

In 1952, the Pittsburgh Pirates signed Pittsburgher Dick Groat after he graduated from Duke. By 1960, he and second basemen Bill Mazeroski were the premier double-play duo in baseball. Groat was the first Pirate to be named MVP since 1927. In the 1960 World Series game seven at Forbes Field, he had an RBI single and scored in the eighth inning, the inning that gave the Pirates a temporary lead. While Groat finished his career in San Francisco, he returned to Pittsburgh for the other sport he excelled at—basketball, and became a broadcaster of University of Pittsburgh basketball, just blocks away from where Forbes Field stood.

By 1960, Forbes Field, perhaps with its last great effort, regularly filled its 36,000 seats for the Pittsburgh Pirates. As the decade moved on, Forbes Field and Philadelphia's Shibe Park were the grand old ladies of major-league ballparks. Pictured above, Forbes Field fit snugly into the expanding University of Pittsburgh property in Oakland.

Forbes Field is pictured at night. Lights were first installed at Forbes Field in 1930, consisting of a jury-rigged standard of floodlights powered by trucks and driven from stadium to stadium. Off in the distance are the neighborhoods across the Monongahela River, Mount Oliver, and Hazelwood at the edge of the Mount Washington ridge.

Fans wait under their umbrellas for the Pittsburgh rain to pass to catch a doubleheader between the Pirates, who were surging to the 1960 pennant, and the Chicago Cubs. The rain did not pass, and the doubleheader was rescheduled to September 22, when the Pirates swept the Cubs. Three days later, the Pirates were National League champions.

While exploits on the field are the focus of fans, there is another side of the story. Behind the men in cleats and caps on Forbes Field grass, there were men in suits and wingtip shoes in Forbes Field offices making the decisions that result in winning teams. For the Pirates, the man who led the men in suits was Joe L. Brown (right), pictured here with shortstop Dick Groat.

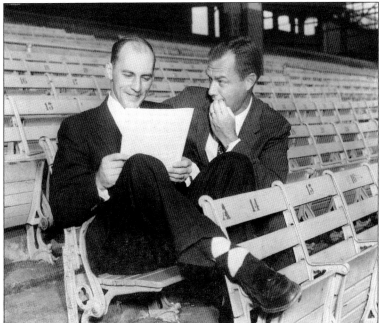

Vernon Law was Pittsburgh's top pitcher in 1960 and the winning pitcher in games one and four of the 1960 World Series. He also started game seven back in Pittsburgh. Law won the Cy Young Award that season, but he was a man and teammate who rose above his statistics. Law was a devout Mormon and lived his creed in what could often be the rough and bawdy world of a professional sports clubhouse. While teammates splashed champagne and beer around the ecstatic Forbes Field clubhouse after beating the great New York Yankees, Law demurred, enjoyed the company of his teammates, and eventually took his celebration over tea and cakes back at his Pittsburgh home with his wife and neighbors.

Bob Friend had a distinguished career as a Pittsburgh Pirate and a leader of baseball's fledgling baseball players union—and enduring pitching on some of the most dreadful teams in the 20th century: the early 1950s Pirates and the infamous 1962 New York Mets. He had a career-high 183 strikeouts in 1960 and his only trip to the World Series.

On October 13, 1960, Bill Mazeroski swung at a pitch left in a dangerous place and took himself, his team, his city, and an aging stadium into history. Decades later, baseball fans whose parents were not even born yet know what the left field wall at Forbes Field looks like, as well as the back of Yogi Berra, who watched the baseball go over it, because of the historic homer.

"Gentleman" George Sisler (left) was a confidant of Pirates general manager Branch Rickey and came to Pittsburgh with him. A tremendous hitter, Sisler hit safely in 41 consecutive games in 1922, creating the American League record that Joe DiMaggio would break 19 years later in 1941. He is pictured here with Don Hoak, who finished second to teammate Dick Groat for National League Most Valuable Player.

When Forbes Field was designed, owner Barney Dreyfuss said he hated "cheap" home runs, so he incorporated a huge outfield to prohibit them. Those huge fields required outfielders who could cover large areas of ground. Bill Virdon was one of those players, as he patrolled the spacious Forbes Field center field magnificently for 11 seasons, winning the Gold Glove in 1962.

In 1959, catcher Forrest Harrill "Smoky" Burgess was traded to the Pirates with Harvey Haddix and Don Hoak. He caught Haddix's May 26, 1959, historic game against the Milwaukee Braves and batted .333 during the 1960 World Series win. Here, Burgess goes after a foul ball along the third base line during the Fall Classic.

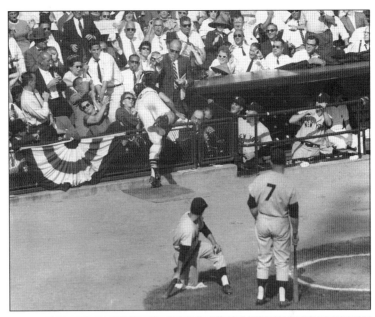

Pictured here is the right field grandstand at Forbes Field in 1960. Ten different players cleared this grandstand (led by Willie Stargell's seven), which stood 86 feet above the field. Babe Ruth was the first to do it, hitting his 714th and last home run in 1935. Others who cleared the roof: Mickey Mantle, Pirates Bob Skinner twice, Eddie Mathews, Rusty Staub, and Willie McCovey.

The story of the finest moment at Forbes Field was a story of the great versus the upstarts—the great New York Yankees versus the upstart Pirates. This was reflected in the two managers, Yankee's Casey Stengel and the Pirates' Danny Murtaugh. Stengel gained fame managing New York teams the Yankees, Dodgers, and Mets, and the New York newspapers made his personality famous. Murtaugh was a very good and hardworking second basemen for the Pirates. In 1957, he was named manager of the franchise, which began a relationship with the Pirates that included four separate stints as skipper, including leading the club to victories in the 1960 and 1971 World Series.

This classic October 1960 image shows Forbes Field in the mid-afternoon, and from the first base foul line, the University of Pittsburgh's Cathedral of Learning reaches to the sky just a few blocks away. The grand old lady of turn-of-the-century ballparks is hosting an improbable World Series in a city that was in a full-swing renaissance that saw a remarkable renovation of the Steel City.

Bill Mazeroski will always be remembered as the man who hit the winning home run in the 1960 World Series at Forbes Field, but if not for Hal Smith, Maz would never have had the chance. In the eighth inning, Smith smacked a pinch-hit three-run homer that gave Pittsburgh a temporary 9-7 lead, setting up Maz's famous hit. Here, manager Danny Murtaugh (left) and Smith celebrate the wild win.

There would be 10 more years of baseball at Forbes Field, but in this photograph, the venerable old park is 90 feet away from becoming an icon. Bill Mazeroski is rounding third and heading for home after hitting a one ball–no strike pitch over the left field fence in Forbes Field to win the 1960 World Series for the Pittsburgh Pirates. When he touched home plate, Oakland and Pittsburgh exploded in joy. Beating the mighty New York Yankees in a seesawing series, at a time when Pittsburgh was renewing itself from a huge mill town to something new, added to the community's elation. It would be 11 years before they captured another series, but the Pittsburgh Pirates were clearly on an upward swing that would continue for two decades.

Six

1961–1970

SAD ENDINGS AND NEW BEGINNINGS

After the magic of 1960, the Pittsburgh Pirates baseball team—like any champion—could either sustain the success, or decline and become a "one-hit wonder."

The Pirates of the mid- to late 1960s took a step back from their 1960 glory year, but the seeds had been planted for a new decade of success with players like Roberto Clemente, Willie Stargell, Donn Clendenon, and others. This is not to say the Pirates were bad; they had some very successful seasons in the 1960s, but it was just the time for other teams to shine.

As was the case in many areas of western culture, the 1960s were a time of evolution and revolution in major-league baseball. The game had migrated to the West Coast and would eventually move north of the border. New York had gone from being home to three clubs to one and would then have two—the Yankees and the woebegone and (eventually) Amazing Mets. The league's hold on players through the reserve clause would be challenged and defeated as players would take their place at the bargaining table.

In Pittsburgh, the renaissance expanded from downtown to neighborhoods as ideas of urban renewal took hold. Pittsburgh's relationship with steel in particular and industry in general expanded and matured.

Meanwhile, these Pirates were playing in what can only fairly be called a shell of its former greatness. Forbes Field was a construct of another era and was giving her all to these Pittsburgh Pirates, while other teams, as the decade was coming to an end, were playing in a new kind of stadium that stressed multiple purposes and had uniformity of size and shape. If the 1960s were a period of expression, that quality was not seen in its sporting venues as the decade was ending.

Catcher Smokey Burgess crosses home with the tying run in the bottom of the ninth against the Philadelphia Phillies at Forbes Field. In the top of the tenth, the Phillies scored, and the Pirates were shut down a half-inning later—win, Philadelphia. At this point in the 1963 season—June 25—the two teams were neck-and-neck in the standings.

In 1963 at Forbes Field, the Pirates got a chance to show off their hardware for the 1962 campaign. Elroy Face was the National League's top relief pitcher as the Fireman of the Year, Bob Bailey was named the Sporting News Minor League Player of the Year, and Roberto Clemente and Bill Virdon won Golden Glove Awards.

There is no greater tradition in major-league baseball than opening day. In the 1960s, opening day at Forbes Field was no different. In its final 11 seasons at Forbes between 1960 and 1970, the team was 7-4 on that special day. Pictured above is the opening day in their world championship season in 1960. That year, the Bucs faced off against the Cincinnati Reds, and Pittsburgh crushed their rivals from the River City at Forbes 13-0. The photograph below is of the Pirates lining up before the 1966 opener against the St. Louis Cardinals. Pittsburgh would not have as much fun at its home park during this opening day, as Bob Gibson hammered the home team with a 9-2 Cardinal win.

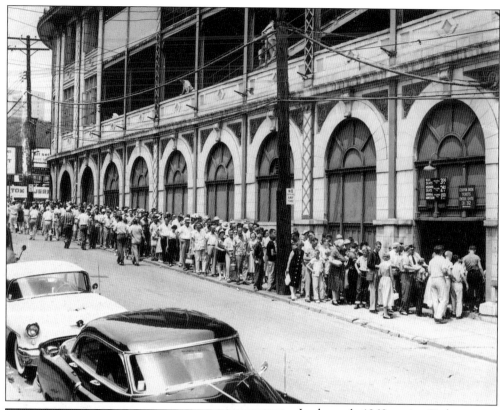

In the early 1960s, aging Forbes Field was still doing year-round duty hosting the Pirates through the spring, summer, and fall, and the NFL's Steelers football team through the fall and winter. In the early 1960s, the Steelers were a hit as crowds lined up to see them. On September 30, 1962, the biggest Steeler crowd ever in Forbes Field history—40,916—watched the Steelers beat the mighty New York Giants.

This is Forbes Field on a quiet night in the university neighborhood of Oakland. Unlike today, with modern parking and transportation systems when fans go to a ball game at Forbes Field, or any other neighborhood ballpark, drivers put their cars where they could and walked. In the foreground, line parking was evidently en vogue at the time, and a quick escape was not in the cards.

Pittsburgh Pirate great Honus Wagner has made the journey with the club. In life, Wagner became one of the first five professional ballplayers inducted in to the Hall of Fame. Wagner won eight batting titles and led the league in slugging six times and in stolen bases five times. His name is spoken with Ty Cobb and Babe Ruth in the pantheon of baseball greats. On April 30, 1955, this statue by Frank Vittor was dedicated and placed in Schenley Park outside the outfield wall of Forbes Field in the Oakland neighborhood of Pittsburgh. In 1972, the statue was rededicated and placed at Gate C of two-year-old Three Rivers Stadium in the North Side of the city. Today, visitors to PNC Park near the former site of Three Rivers find Wagner's statue first among the great Pirates depicted in bronze around the park.

Pirates shortstop Gene Alley crosses home plate at Forbes Field during a game against the St. Louis Cardinals during the closing season of the venerable old ballyard. As the Pirates improved through the late 1960s and into the 1970s, the Cardinals were persistent rivals, as both teams featured a balance of strong pitching, hitting, and speed.

If Roberto Clemente became a star and eventually an icon in the early 1970s, it was in the 1960s that his legend was born. After inconsistent seasons, starting in 1955, Clemente hit his stride in 1960, when his batting average ballooned to .314 and remained over .300 throughout the decade, except for 1968. He combined his offensive prowess with one of the greatest defensive abilities the game has ever seen.

This team photograph comes at the start of the 1970 season. That campaign began in the 61st year in the life of Forbes Field and would end in the newly built Three Rivers Stadium. Baseball would move from the close-in neighborhood of Oakland to the comparatively open space of the North Shore of the Allegheny River. While the venue would change, and shortly after that, the uniforms, the core of players depicted here would not, becoming world champions a year later. Pictured are some important members from the soon-to-be champs, including, from left to right, (first row; first, ninth, and eleventh, respectively) Jose Pagan, Al Oliver, and Manny Sanguillen; (second row; first, seventh, eighth, and tenth, respectively) Roberto Clemente, Bob Robertson, Willie Stargell, and Steve Blass; (third row; first and fifth, respectively) Bill Mazeroski and Dock Ellis.

There had not been a single no-hitter at Forbes Field—despite the fact it was a pitchers' park, one of the great facts of the facility—until 1971, when Bob Gibson tossed a gem for the Cardinals at Three Rivers Stadium; Pittsburgh fans had gone 64 years without seeing one. The closest anyone had come was in 1968 when Bob Moose (below) of Export, Pennsylvania, went 7 2/3 no-hit innings against Houston before giving up a single to Julio Gotay in the eighth on his way to a two-hitter. A year later at New York, he threw a no-hitter, beating the eventual World Series winners, the Mets. Moose died on his 29th birthday in an auto accident on October 9, 1976.

Getting seats close up at Forbes Field meant keeping one's eye on the game. The large spaces between foul lines and stands often meant catchers would be able to get to foul balls. Here, an opposing catcher runs out of space as he gets up close and personal with fans on the third base side of Forbes Field.

Fans beat a retreat from their field seats at Forbes Field as it rains during a game in Pittsburgh. In the 1960s, unless a person lived in Houston after the Astrodome was built in 1965, it did not matter if the baseball venue was a year old or decades old; baseball remains an outdoor game subject to the whims of nature.

Oakland has gone through a lot of changes since the Pirates left Forbes Field as the sprawling University of Pittsburgh campus swallowed up the property, but Gus Miller's Newsstand at 3801 Forbes Avenue remains. It opened in 1909, the same year as the ballpark, and was located across the street. Along with running the newsstand, Miller was the head usher at Forbes Field. (Courtesy of David Finoli.)

This photograph shows the changing face of Oakland. The Litchfield Towers, freshman dormitories for Pitt students known to this day as A, B, and C, were built in 1963 and house over 1,800 students. It is part of a complex of Pitt student services, offices, and food courts that are the social center of the lower Pitt campus. The complex is located across from where Forbes Field stood. (Courtesy of David Finoli.)

Since the 1950s, the Pirates and the city had discussed a new ballpark. The University of Pittsburgh bought Forbes Field in 1958, and its demise was expected to be imminent. A series of plans emerged for a new, multipurpose stadium (such as the one pictured above) that could be used by the Pirates as well as the Pittsburgh Steelers, who were playing in Pitt Stadium. By 1970, Three Rivers Stadium (below) was completed and opened for business. This was the new fashion. Multipurpose structures were utilitarian in nature, convertible from a baseball to a football configuration, but not particularly optimized for either sport. The coziness of Forbes Field was replaced with great slabs of reinforced concrete and surrounded by asphalt fields for parking. Placing the stadium at the confluence of the Allegheny, Monongahela, and Ohio Rivers was part of the larger plan to focus attention on the downtown Golden Triangle.

As Forbes Field's tenure was coming to a close in 1970, the park became the object of curiosity and memories. Here, students and neighborhood kids scale the outfield wall and walk the field their heroes had walked for years. Notice the batting cage that was stored by the wall in the spacious center field has collapsed in the melee and is being protected by the police. A few months after this photograph was taken, Forbes Field forever shut its doors after 40,918 patrons showed up on June 28, 1970, to see the Pirates sweep the Cubs almost 61 years from the day it opened.

Seven

1971–Present
The Years Since

So impressive was Forbes Field when it opened on June 30, 1909, *The Pittsburgh Press* said that the citizens of the city could "boast of the world's finest baseball park. It is a marvel of which people in other cities can have no adequate conception until they come here and see it."

It was a magnificent facility that was the scene of many great moments in its 61 years. Unfortunately, as the 1960s came and passed, this once legendary park was beaten down and was about to give way.

The powers that be were building a sparkling new facility in the North Side of Pittsburgh, on the shores where the three rivers meet, ironically only a few feet away from where Exposition Park—the stadium that prompted Barney Dreyfuss to move his team to the Oakland section of the city because of flooding— stood 61 years earlier. In the 1970s, flooding was no longer a concern on the North Side, and Three Rivers Stadium opened its doors in 1970.

Two fires in the early 1970s at a barren Forbes Field all but destroyed it, and demolition began in 1971 to make room for Wesley Posvar Hall. It was all taken down, except for a section of the outfield wall that would remain to this day.

In 1985, a yearly event began to take shape when Saul Finklestien, sick of the losing ways of the Pirates at that point, decided to celebrate the 25th anniversary of Mazeroski's famous 1960 home run by taking his radio to the wall and listening to the rebroadcast. As the years went on, his annual sojourn became more and more popular. By 2010, the 50-year anniversary, Finklestien's one-man tribute became a city celebration as over 1,000 fans came to the wall as it was covered by MLB Network and attended by many of the living members of the 1960 team.

The wall has now become a point where fans can relive the glory of this legendary park.

What used to be the site of Forbes Field is today Wesley Posvar Hall on the campus of the University of Pittsburgh. Named after the school's former chancellor, Posvar Hall is home to the Graduate School of Public and International Affairs, the University Center for International Studies, the Social Sciences Departments, and the Undergraduate College of Business Administration. Posvar Hall also houses mementos of the stadium that used to occupy these very grounds. Several photographs of the facility surround its walls as well as a plaque commemorating the final doubleheader played at Forbes against the Cubs in 1970. Most importantly, home plate is encased on the floor not far from the exact place that it was at when the field was open. (Both, courtesy of David Finoli.)

To the right of where the home base entrance would have been, towards the first baseline, now sits the Barco Law Building at the University of Pittsburgh. Built for $8.5 million, the Barco Law Building was part of the Pitt expansion that happened after Forbes Field was demolished, and it was opened in January 1976. The building was named in memory of George Barco and his daughter Yolanda, who were both graduates of the Pitt Law School. The building includes a massive three-floor law library that has over 325,000 volumes and the Teplitz Memorial Moot Courtroom, which is used primarily for trial tactics classes and moot court programs. (Courtesy of David Finoli.)

Near where the right field wall and right field grandstand as well as the first base grandstand used to sit is Mervis Hall, where the nationally renowned Joseph Katz Graduate School of Business resides. Named after generous donor, alumnus, and former football star Lou Mervis, who played at Forbes under legendary coach Pop Warner, Mervis Hall was built and dedicated in 1983 to house the Katz School of Business. The business school was established in 1960 and was recently ranked 11th in the country among public business schools by the Princeton Review. It was also ranked in the top 10 affordable high-quality programs in the country. (Both, courtesy of David Finoli.)

A youth baseball field, located where the left field wall of Forbes Field once stood, is named after the man who gave Forbes its most memorable moment, Bill Mazeroski. Even though Forbes is no longer there, the memories in the minds of Steel City sports fans will always be there. The field played host to four National League championships, two World Series titles, three national championships for Pitt, several boxing titles, and even the classic 1951 film *Angels in the Outfield*. These memories and more keep this facility alive in the minds of those it touched. (Courtesy of David Finoli.)

While the facility is gone, what remains to this day are the outfield flag pole and part of the brick wall, so Pittsburgh sports fans still have a piece of Forbes Field to hold onto. The wall that stands behind Posvar Hall was the last of several walls that were erected during the tenure of Forbes Field. The first ones were made of wood, but this brick one did not come about until 1946, when new owner John Galbreath had it installed. What is common today was not in the 1940s, when crash pads were put on the right and right center field walls to protect the outfielders. (Both, courtesy of David Finoli.)

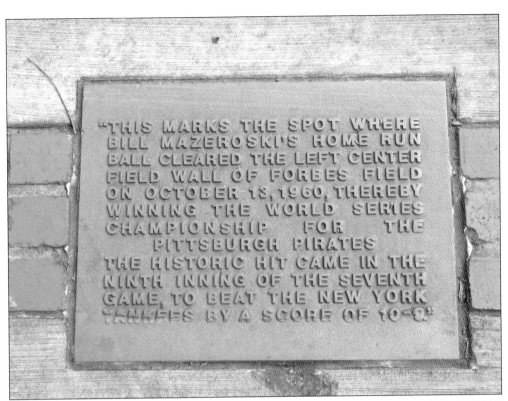

"THIS MARKS THE SPOT WHERE BILL MAZEROSKI'S HOME RUN BALL CLEARED THE LEFT CENTER FIELD WALL OF FORBES FIELD ON OCTOBER 13, 1960, THEREBY WINNING THE WORLD SERIES CHAMPIONSHIP FOR THE PITTSBURGH PIRATES THE HISTORIC HIT CAME IN THE NINTH INNING OF THE SEVENTH GAME, TO BEAT THE NEW YORK YANKEES BY A SCORE OF 10-9"

Part of the wall that did not survive was the left field one where Bill Mazeroski hit his majestic home run in game seven of the 1960 World Series to win the game and the championship for the Pirates 10-9. One of the greatest moments in the history of the city of Pittsburgh is commemorated today by a plaque (above), which was placed exactly where the ball flew over the wall on that memorable day. There is a brick line that leads up to Posvar Hall (right) where the remainder of the Forbes Field wall once stood. (Both, courtesy of David Finoli.)

Above, a Pennsylvania State Historical Marker, where Forbes Field used to stand, commemorates the exciting events and memories that took place during its 61-year history. While the plaque fails to give credit to the great Duquesne and Carnegie Tech football teams that graced its field, it does celebrate just about everything else that was special about it. (Courtesy of David Finoli.)

In the lower floor of Posvar Hall is the encased home plate that was used at Forbes Field. While it is close, it is not in the exact spot that it stood when players like Roberto Clemente and Honus Wagner were looking down pitchers' eyes. The actual spot, located in a nearby restroom, is approximately 10 feet from where this one is. (Courtesy of David Finoli.)

There is a celebration annually at the Forbes Field wall on October 13, beginning at around 1:00 p.m. and ending at exactly 3:36 p.m. The celebration is the radio rebroadcast of game seven of the 1960 World Series. Every year, hundreds of Pirate faithful show up, like author and baseball historian Bill Ranier (left) and Dennis Gilfoyle. (Courtesy of David Finoli.)

On October 13, 2010, Pirate fans packed the Forbes Field wall to celebrate the 50th anniversary of arguably the greatest World Series home run of all time—Bill Mazeroski's ninth-inning shot against the Yankees to win the 1960 World Championship. Many of the living members of that special team were in attendance that day to relive the pinnacle of their careers. (Courtesy of David Finoli.)

For the 50th anniversary of Bill Mazeroski's legendary home run in the 1960 World Series, the City of Pittsburgh, Pirate Charities, and the Pittsburgh Parks Conservancy decided to give Maz yet another one of the many honors bestowed upon him to commemorate what is one of the most electric moments in the long history of sports in the Steel City with this plaque in the ground on the sidewalk going to the Forbes Field wall. While he was most well known for his home run, Mazeroski was one of the greatest second baseman defensively in the annals of the game. His defense was the primary reason he was elected to the Baseball Hall of Fame in 2001. (Both, courtesy of David Finoli.)

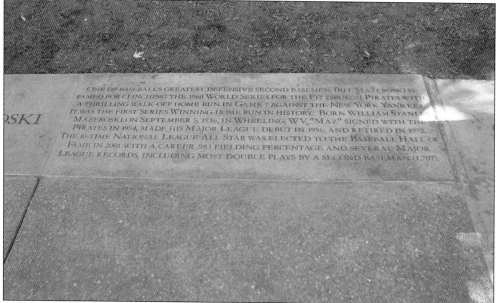

To further celebrate what was one of the most special ballparks in the history of baseball, the members of the Carpenters District Council built a replica of the Forbes Field entrance gate and ticket window in 2006. The replica is built behind the Forbes Field wall right next to a youth baseball park, Mazeroski Field, named for the legendary second baseman. (Courtesy of David Finoli.)

This section of the Forbes Field wall, part of the 406-foot left center field, was taken and displayed in the Allegheny Club at Three Rivers Stadium. This important piece of memorabilia was stored after Three Rivers was imploded and was finally restored in 2009, where it is displayed at the river walk at PNC Park behind the Bill Mazeroski statue. (Courtesy of David Finoli.)

DISCOVER THOUSANDS OF LOCAL HISTORY BOOKS FEATURING MILLIONS OF VINTAGE IMAGES

Arcadia Publishing, the leading local history publisher in the United States, is committed to making history accessible and meaningful through publishing books that celebrate and preserve the heritage of America's people and places.

Find more books like this at
www.arcadiapublishing.com

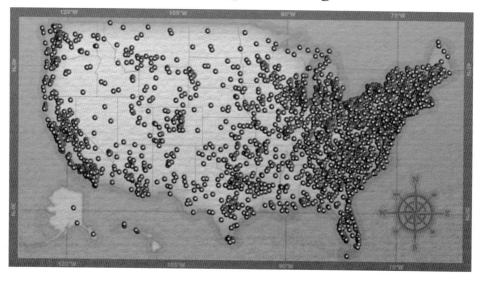

Search for your hometown history, your old stomping grounds, and even your favorite sports team.

Consistent with our mission to preserve history on a local level, this book was printed in South Carolina on American-made paper and manufactured entirely in the United States. Products carrying the accredited Forest Stewardship Council (FSC) label are printed on 100 percent FSC-certified paper.

MADE IN THE USA